KEY WEST, FLORIDA, USA, 1968.

LONDON, ENGLAND, 1966

PROVENCE, FRANCE, 1958

NO

DOGS

PARIS FRANCE 1956

BIRMINGHAM, ENGL

ST. TROPEZ FRANCE 1970

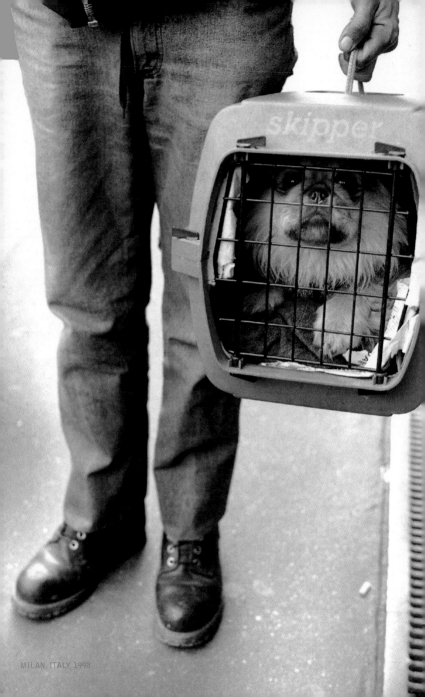

MILAN, ITALY, 1998

NICE, FRANCE, 1951

SOUTH CAROLINA

ST. TROPEZ, FRANCE, 1979

PARIS

NEW YORK, NY, USA, 1974

TOKYO, JAPAN, 1985

BRIGHTON

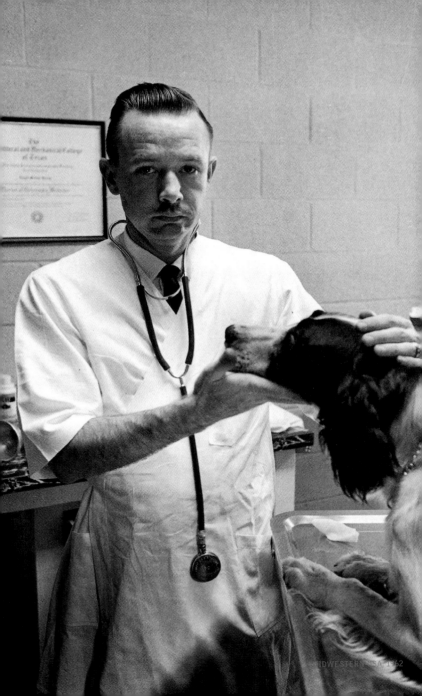

KYOTO, JAPAN 1970

NEW MEXICO USA, 1962

NEW YORK, NY, USA, 1995

CANNES, FRANCE, 1989

DEAUVILLE, FRANCE, 1965

PARIS, FRANCE, 1966

NORMANDY, FRANCE, 1995

ZURICH, SWITZERLAND, 1991

ST. TROPEZ, FRANCE, 1979

MIDDLETON, IRELAND. 1976

Au Chrysanthème

Monuments Funéraires - Fleurs Plastiques

HONFLEUR, FRANCE, 1968

NORTH VIETNAM 1994

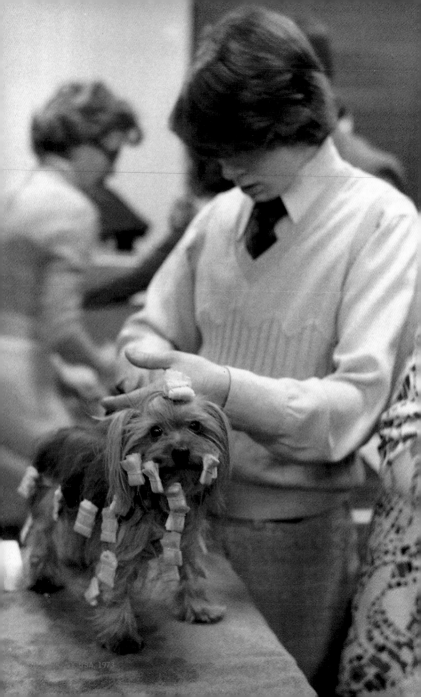

ROME, I

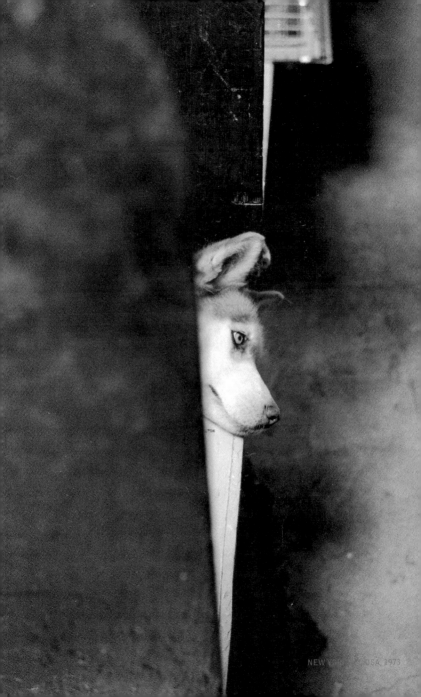

WASHINGTON, D.C., USA, 1965

LONDON, ENGLAND, 1968

FRENCH COUNTRYSIDE/1984

ST. TROPEZ, FRANCE, 1968

SAN JUAN, PUERTO

NASSAU·BAHAMAS, 1967

ZURICH, SWITZERLAND, 1991

FAIRBANKS, AK, USA, 1966

BALLYCOTTON, IRELAND, 1970

BALLYCOTTON, IRELAND, 1968

LUXOR EGYPT 1958

VIENNA, AUSTRIA, 1958

RIO DE JANEIRO, BRAZIL; 1963

SHANAGARRY, IRELAND, 1982

ARENAL, MEXICO, 1952

NORMANDY FRANCE 1999

BERLIN GERMANY 1995

MYKONOS GREECE 1976

EAST HAMPTON, NY USA

MILAN, ITALY, 1949

MILAN, ITALY, 1990

GUARD
ROOM

ACAPULCO, MEXICO 1991

BERLIN, GERMANY, 1995

TROUVILLE FRANCE

USA, 1972

BERLIN, GERMANY, 1995

NEW YORK, NY, USA, 1977

ST-TROPEZ, FRANCE, 1979

KYOTO, JAPAN, 1977

TOKYO, JAPAN 19

DRINKS
GROCERIES
OPALS
SAPHIRES
TOPAZ
AGATE
PETRIFIED
WOOD
CRYSTAL
WATER
AMETHYST
GARNETS

...gs Taken
...re

COOBER PEDY, AUSTRALIA, 1972

LONDON, ENGLAND, 1970

CLOYNE, IRELAND

BIRMINGHAM, ENGLAND, 1991

My Dog Days   Elliott Erwitt

The original concept for this book was to include 1000 dogs and one cat. But as the days grew longer in preparation, the number of dogs grew shorter and I managed to squeeze only 820 dogs (and a few cats for balance) into these 512 pages. Be assured, dear reader, that my collection of pooches over the past 50 years far exceeds a mere thousand. Starting with my first published Chihuahua, photographed in New York in 1946, to my last mongrel taken in Ayutthaya in 1998, I hope to have assembled a representative number and variety of man and woman's most enduring and loyal friends worldwide.

My attraction to dogs is stirred purely by emotion. The romance started in the mid-1940s when, as a lonely teenager growing up in Hollywood, California, I adopted a shabby, nondescript, but exceptionally intelligent and sensitive mutt who was suffering from life-threatening canine distemper. Old Terry did pull through and recover after massive intervention from the local veterinarian at my insistent urging when a *coup de grace* might have been more appropriate. His physical appearance declined even further during the convalescence but his intelligence and sensitivity grew.

I guess suffering humbles and enriches. He was one lovable mess. Our relationship was one of mutual respect and interdependence. He continued to be a street dog but one who always came home whenever it seemed appropriate. . . and not just to be fed. Terry was friendly to my neighbours along Fountain Avenue and often accompanied the postman on his rounds. When the spirit moved him, Terry used to visit my mother who lived several miles away in the eastern part of Hollywood. All on his own, Terry would cross streets and boulevards, dodge traffic and always find his way there and back. Terry's only vice was a meek chasing of the occasional bicycle – unconvincing at best in his reduced condition.

with dogs, as in love affairs, the first and the last are the most vivid. Terry has been in dog heaven for about seven dog generations. There have been just a few interim *cani familiaris* in my life due to its essentially vagrant nature with my peripatetic travels, all of them very nice and *familiari* but none especially remarkable. That is, until the recent arriva of Sammy.

Sammy is a Hamburg-born cairn terrier of prope breeding and worldly demeanor. An essential cosmopolite having travelled extensively through Europe and transatlantically a half-dozen times, he came in to my life a few years ago with my zweedheardt Pia and her son Jonny. Sammy is a sophisticated, socially apt and wilfully opinionated little beast (you'll see his political statement on the Brandenburg Gate in Berlin and his general attitude on this essay's opening spread). We like each other but he doesn't go overboard and make a federal case of it, as say a golden lab would. Ou modus vivendi is mutual respect and an awareness of one another's boundaries.

Sammy and I have the start of an as-yet-unrealized projec or which we are seeking corporate or art-foundatio sponsorship. That is, to travel and repeat the Brandenburg statement upon every other important pompous monument in he world, except for Britain where the six-month dog quarantine would be make our scheme unworkable. Imagine he scope of our plan. Sammy marking the Arc de Triomphe in Paris, the Coliseum in Rome, the Statue of Liberty in Nev York, the Royal Palace in Bangkok, the Pyramids of Giza in Egypt, the Lenin Mausoleum in Moscow's Red Square, the Gateway to the Forbidden City in Beijing and so on and on What magnificent gestures. I guess we can dream.

Like Sammy, dogs don't mind being photographed in

compromising situations, which is not to say that dogs are ever self-conscious. In fact, a cruel person, or a photographer could easily embarrass them. But they are usually unaffected because of their innocence, and lack of guile. Perhaps that's why dogs seem to have a natural bond with children. Maybe they still have some fundamental values that haven't been corrupted by society.

Dogs are not exactly like children, though. They are more nonchalant. They don't necessarily want you to notice that they are around, because they know that they belong. Dogs don't have to say "Look at me!" the way children often do. However, they are more unfocussed than children. For one thing, they are forced to lead a life that is really schizoid. Every day they must live on two planes at once, juggling the dog world with the human world. And they're always on call. Their owners demand constant affection every day, any time of day. A dog can never say that he has a headache or other things to do.

I am a professional photographer by trade and an amateur photographer by vocation. Most of the time when I am out of the house I carry a small unobtrusive camera and I snap away obsessively at things that interest me and whatever I think would make a good picture. Until recently, I have never especially set out to take dog pictures but somehow dogs appeared in large numbers on my contact sheets. A few years back while looking through my inventory of pictures to assemble a retrospective book and exhibition of random photographs taken on my travels, I was surprised by the preponderance of dogs. Obviously my sympathy for the creatures was deeper than I had imagined.

Many of the dogs pictured must have looked appealing to me in their exotic settings, other dogs were appealing in reasonably well-composed photographs and some other seemed to transcend their easy obvious charm and to have allegorical connotations to us humans and to our human condition. As I think about this now, my comments don't sound particularly surprising. I don't know of any other animals closer to us in qualities of heart, sentiment and loyalty. Some people say elephants come close. Personally, I find elephants too bulky, unwieldy and inaccessible for everyday photography and not at all cuddly or attractive with those big long noses. Besides, they do not roam the streets in every town and every country like dogs do. And dogs make easy, uncomplaining targets without the self-conscious hang-ups and possible objections of humans caught on film.

Because of my growing dog inventory I have become increasingly sensitised to the omnipresence of pooches everywhere I travel and so I have been throwing my psychic and photographic frame around them, manipulating their image inside of my geometric mean, organizing the compositions and attempting to make them my own.

And so we have the result in this volume. If dog-lovers think this is a dog book, that's all right with me. Especially if they buy extra copies for their dog-loving friends. One of these little guys might remind you of a dog you know, or used to know. That's fine too.

For me, the dogs are both an excuse and a reason for taking these pictures. They give me an excuse because they make good subjects. I like them, people want to see them, I can't resist!

In the end, this is not a book of dog pictures but of dogs in pictures.

This edition published by Barnes & Noble, Inc.,
by arrangement with Phaidon Press Limited

© 1998 Phaidon Press Limited
Photographs © 1998 Elliott Erwitt/Magnum Photos
2000 Barnes & Noble Books

ISBN
0-7607-2303-6

About my Friends by P.G. Wodehouse reproduced with the permission
of A.P. Watt on behalf of the trustees of the Wodehouse Estate

A CIP catalogue record of
this book is available from
the British Library.

Printed in Singapore

M 10 9 8 7 6 5 4 3 2 1

called on me to say his ducks were disappearing and suspicion had fallen on my Rudolph. Why? I asked, and he said because mine was the only dog in the vicinity except his own Towser, and Towser had been so carefully trained that he would not touch a duck if you brought it to him with orange sauce over it.

I was indignant. I said he had only to gaze into Rudolph's candid brown eyes to see how baseless were his suspicions. Had he not, I asked, heard of foxes? Or weasels? Or stoats? How much more likely that one of these was the Bad Guy in the sequence? He was beginning to waver and seemed on the verge of an apology, when Rudolph, who had been listening with the greatest interest and at a certain point had left the room, came trotting in with a duck in his mouth.

Yes, dachshunds overplay their sense of humour, and I suppose other dogs have their defects, but they seem trivial compared with their merits. So put down that camera, Mr. Erwitt, and join me in a standing ovation to all dogs, whether Airedale, wire-haired terriers, bulldogs, Pekinese, cairns, spaniels, pugs, Maltese, Yorkshires, borzois, bloodhounds, Bedlingtons, pointers, setters, mastiffs, Newfoundlands, St. Bernards, Great Danes, collies, chows, poodles, and those peculiar little Mexican dogs beginning with C and sounding like a sneeze.

...ng was very like the big scene in one of those in which
where the prison personnel are trying to persuade James
Cagney to enter the death chamber. Eventually, after man
days, he decided his fears had been ill-founded and we were al
able to relax.

The question of whether dogs have a sense of humour is
often hotly debated, and I should like to take it up with Mr
Erwitt next time he has a moment. My own opinion is tha
some have and some don't. Dachshunds have, but not St
Bernards and Great Danes. It would seem that a dog has to be
small to be fond of a joke. You never find an Irish wolfhoun
trying to be a stand-up comic.

But it is fatal to let any dog know that he is funny, for he
immediately loses his head and starts hamming it up. As an
instance of this I would point to Rudolph, a dachshund I once
owned, whose slogan was Anything for a Laugh. Dachshund
are always the worst offenders in this respect because of thei
peculiar shape. It is only natural that when a dog finds that hi
mere appearance makes the viewing public giggle, he shoul
assume that Nature intended him for a comedian's role.

I had a cottage at the time outside an English village, no
far from a farm where they kept ducks, and one day the farme

course. For centuries they belonged only to Emperors. If you were not an Emperor and were found with a Peke on your premises, you got the Death Of a Thousand Cuts, an old Chinese punishment for minor offences roughly equivalent to our fifteen-dollar fine for parking next to a fire plug. But none of our Pekes pulled rank on us. They could not have been more democratic and affable. And how Mr. Elliott Erwitt would have loved to photograph them.

Over Bill the foxhound, the first of our Remsenburg dogs, even Mr. Erwitt, broadminded though he is, would, I'm afraid, have shaken his head. Bill was a stray in the last stages of starvation and so covered with ticks that only the keenest eye could detect that there was a dog underneath.

Taken in and fed and nursed and scientifically de-ticked, he soon settled down – but only in the country. Came a time when he had to come with us to New York, when, alighting from the car, he refused to enter the apartment house, evidently suspecting a trap. I dragged him as far as the elevator, and again he jibbed. I finally got him on board, and he then refused to emerge. No doubt he thought that while conditions in the elevator were pretty bad, they were nothing to the horrors which lurked behind that sinister apartment door. The whole any child who collected a quarter thought he had done well.

When Sammy succumbed to old age, I made what I think was a mistake by appointing as his successor an Aberdeen terrier who was supposed (though he seldom did) to answer to the name of Angus. Aberdeen terriers are intelligent and (if you don't mind those beetling eyebrows) handsome, but so austere and full of the Calvinistic spirit that it is impossible for an ordinary erring human being not to feel ill at ease in their presence. Angus had a way of standing in front of me and looking at me like a Scottish preacher about to rebuke the sins of his congregation. Sundays with him were particularly trying. There is almost nothing you can do on a Sunday which does not arouse the disapproval of an Aberdeen terrier. He would grudgingly consent to come with me for a walk after lunch, but if I so forgot myself as to whistle for him, his manner plainly showed what his opinion was of people so sunk in sin as to whistle on the Sabbath. It was a relief when I gave him to a better man than myself.

After Angus my wife and I fell under the spell of Pekes. Many people, I know, disparage Pekes, but take it from me, they are all right. If they have a fault, it is a tendency to think too much of themselves. One can readily understand it, of are. It does one good to look at them. There is not a sitter in his gallery who does not melt the heart. And no beastly class distinctions, either. Thoroughbred or mutts, they are all here.

What with one thing and another it was not till I went to live at Great Neck, Long Island, that I actually owned a dog of my own. Guy Bolton, Jerry Kern and I were writing a revue for Flo Ziegfeld at that time. It did only thirty-seven performances, so the pickings were none too good, but I was able to save something out of the wreck, for one of the company gave me a French bulldog called Sammy, as amiable and sweet-natured an animal as ever broke biscuit. Too amiable, we sometimes used to feel. He was always liking the looks of passers-by outside our garden gate and trotting out to fraternize with them. The first time he disappeared I gave the man who brought him back ten dollars, and this got around among the local children and stirred up their business instincts. They would come to our gate and call, "Sammy, Sammy, Sammy," and old Sam would waddle along and they would bring him back with a cheery "We found your dog wandering down the road, mister," and cash in. Obviously no purse could stand the drain, especially with revues running for only thirty-seven performances. The bottom dropped out of the market, and it was not long before

About my Friends P.G. Wodehouse

We all have plenty to say about dogs, but very seldom are we allowed to say it. One of the familiar sights at any cocktail party is that of a man — call him Man A — trying to tell another man — call him Man B — all about the intelligence of his dog and the other man cutting in and starting to tell him all about the intelligence of *his* dog; whereupon Man A raises his voice and Man B raises his voice until both are bringing plaster down from the ceiling and giving bystanders the impression that they have wandered into a student protest demonstration. It is estimated by statisticians that more pique, umbrage, dudgeon, and bad blood are engendered in this way than by any other method of engendering p, u, d, and bb. True, blows are seldom exchanged, but these encounters nearly always lead to the ending of friendships.

How wise, then, of Mr. Elliott Erwitt to avoid those vulgar brawls and stick to photographing dogs instead of talking about them. No agony for him of being shouted down by some uncouth moron with a louder voice. And what superb photographs his

YORK, NY, USA 1987

PUERTO VALLARTA, MEXICO, 1973

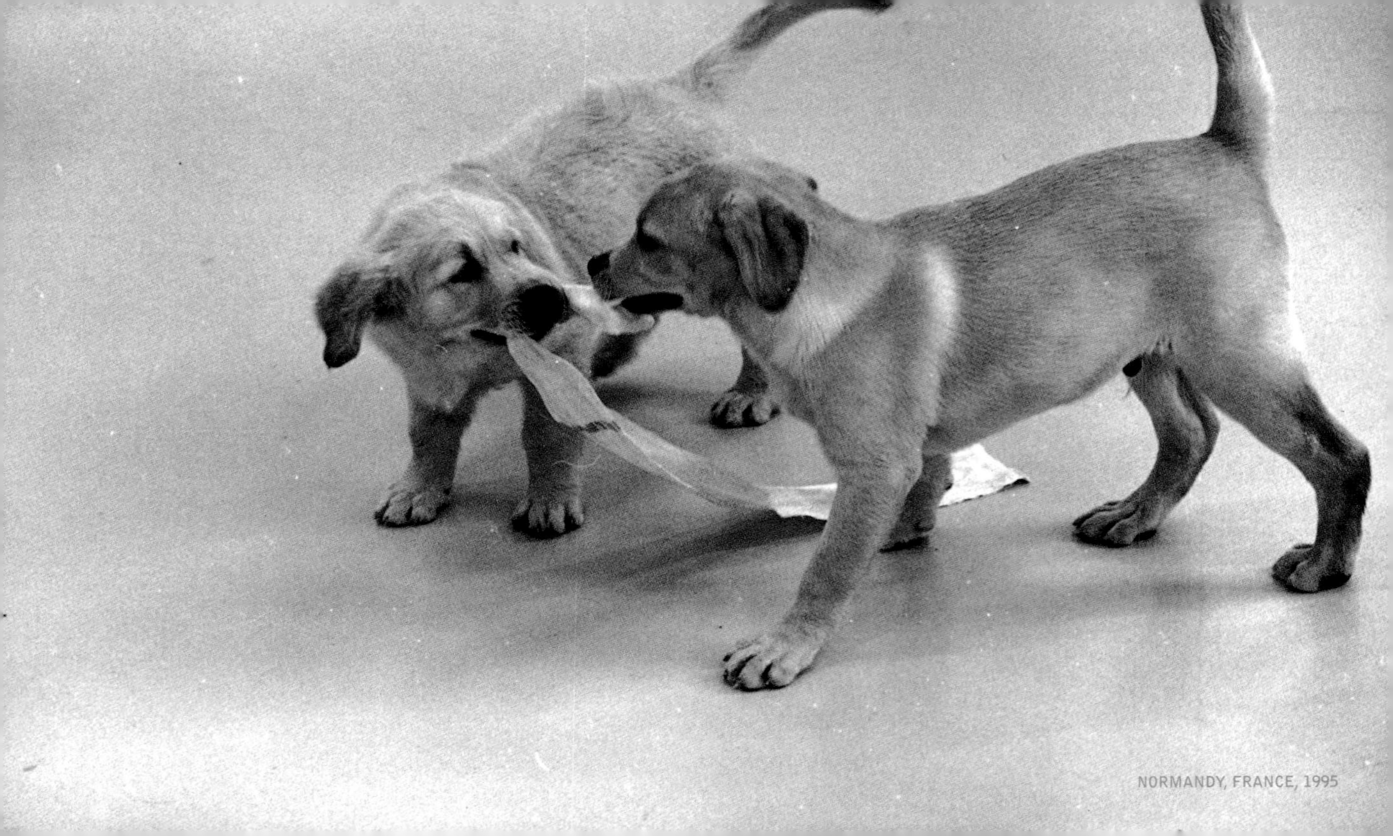

NORMANDY, FRANCE, 1995

NORMANDY, FRANCE, 1995

BIRMINGHAM, ENGLAND, 1991

MILAN, ITALY, 1990

MIDWESTERN USA, 1963

PARIS, FRANCE, 19

NEW YORK, NY, USA, 1990

PARIS, FRANCE, 19

SYLT, GERMANY, 1996

ROME, ITALY 1978

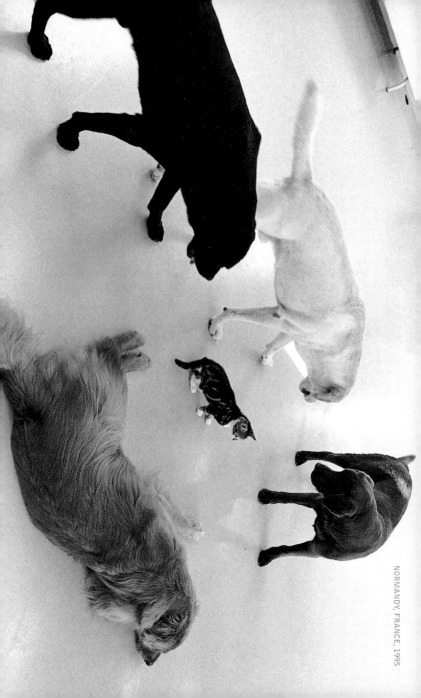

NORMANDY FRANCE, 1995

BANGKOK, THAILAND 1998

BERLIN, GERMANY, 1995

IRELAND, 1970

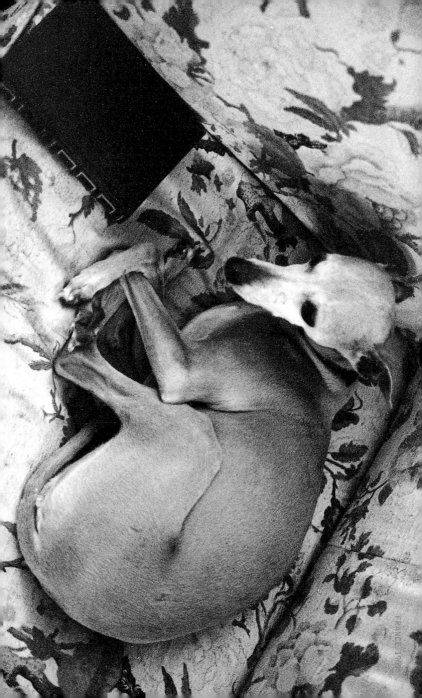

FRANCE 199

NEW YORK, NY, USA, 1972

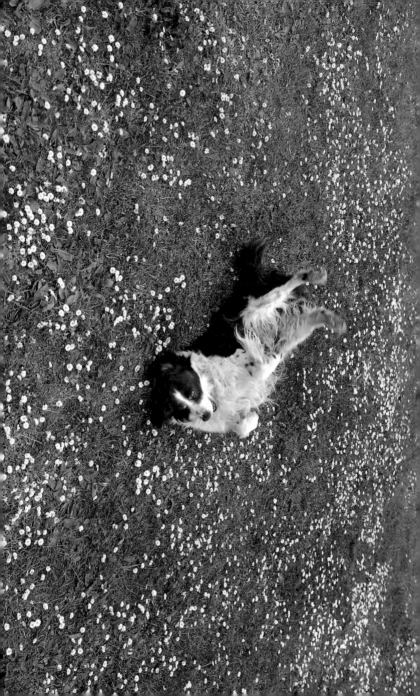

BERLIN, GERMANY, 1995

ST. TROPEZ, FRANCE, 1979

SOUTHERN FRANCE 1978

SOUTHAMPTON, NY, USA, 1969

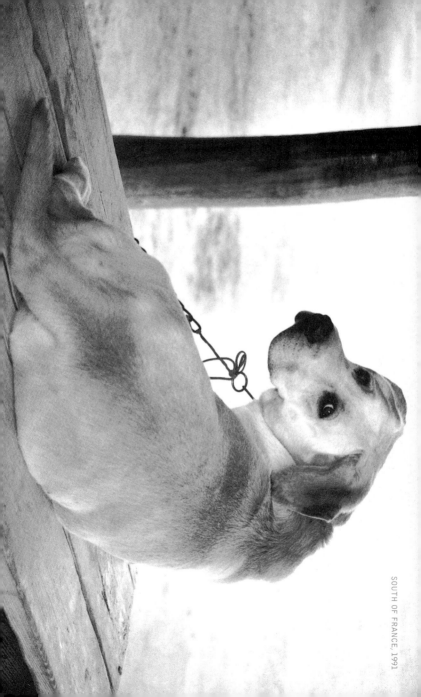

STINSON BEACH, CA, USA, 1973

BERLIN, GERMANY 1995

BUENOS AIRES – ARGENTINA 1972

SAN FRANCISCO, CA, USA, 1975

AMAGANSETT, NY, USA, 1990

NEW YORK NY USA 1955

SOUTHERN FRANCE, 1978

BRIDGEHAMPTON, NY, USA, 1990

BÚZIOS, BRAZIL, 1990

BUZIOS, BRAZIL, 1990

ST. TROPEZ, FRANCE, 1970

USA 1964

AMAGANSETT, N.Y. USA, 1997

VENICE CA USA 1986

LONDON, ENGLAND, 1968

HONFLEUR, FRANCE, 1968

MALIBU CA USA 1962

ZURICH, SWITZERLAND, 1991

CORNWALL, ENGLAND, 1974

ST. TROPEZ, FRANCE, 1979

FRANCE, 1991

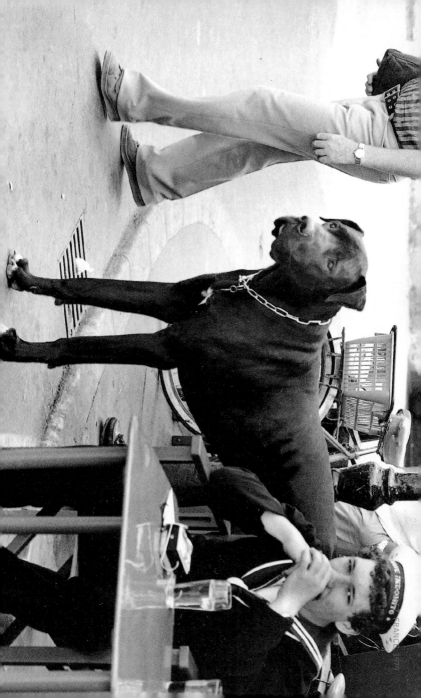

"LONDON JACK"
THE ORPHANAGE FRIEND.
THIS DOG FROM 1894 TO 1900.
COLLECTED FOR THE L.& S.W.R. Servants
Orphanage £250 & the other Charitable
objects about £200

All Contributions deposited in this Box
will be gratefully received and placed
to Jack's credit in the recovery in
the above manner Charity

LONDON
JACK

MOTOR RACING
AT
GOODWOOD

TER MONDAY, MARCH 30th
WHIT MONDAY, MAY 18th
ATURDAY, AUGUST 29th

EAP TICKETS
ISSUED
M THIS STATION
TO
HICHESTER

DETAILS OF FARES AND TRAIN SERVICES

VIETNAM, 1994

NORMANDY, FRANCE, 1995

SOUTHERN IRELAND, 1982

MOSCOW, RUSSIA 1968

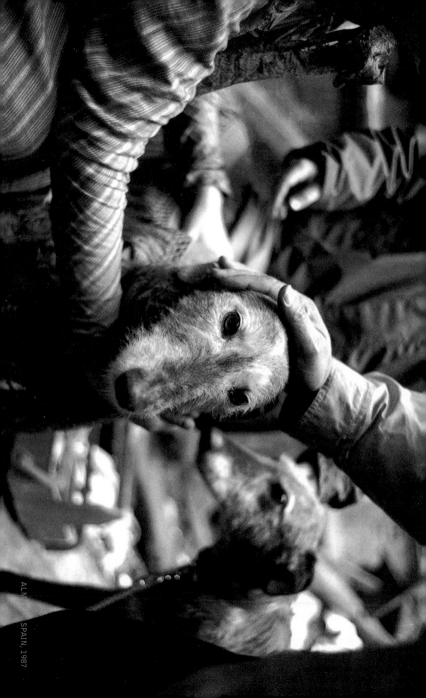

ST-TROPEZ GE 1979

ENGLAND, 1974

NEW YORK, NY, USA, 1973

DEAUVILLE, FRANCE, 1991